WOOD PELLET GRILL AND SMOKER COOKBOOK

COMPLETE SMOKER COOKBOOK FOR REAL PITMASTERS, THE ULTIMATE GUIDE FOR SMOKING MEAT, FISH, GAME AND VEGETABLES

DANIEL MURRAY

TABLE OF CONTENTS

INTRODUCTION

Through history, smoking been a preferred way of preserving food, but it so much more than just a way to keep food from going bad! Smoking also introduces complex and delicious flavors into dishes that are otherwise often bland or uninteresting. In modern cooking, it's a great way to mix up staples in your home cooking, and it can be a really fantastic way to wow people at a potluck, or to host an incredible dinner party. Smoking is not only inventive and delicious, it also makes it really easy to make large quantities of food at the same time without too much fuss. Traditionally, smoking is done by burning wood chips in a small enclosed area with the food, allowing the food to be cooked very slowly, while absorbing the rich smoky flavor. Today, smoking is often associated with sports tail-gaiting parties and small family get-togethers. This guide is designed to both embrace that culture, and also offer up some techniques and recipes that will let you take your smoking to the next level: full-blown gourmet food full of layered and nuanced deliciousness.

CHAPTER 1: BEEF RECIPES

STRIP STEAK SMOKED AND SEARED

(COOKING TIME: 3 HOURS 10 MINUTES)

INGREDIENTS FOR 4 SERVINGS

- Strip streaks – 2 (At least 1" thick)
- Olive oil – 2 teaspoon
- Kosher salt to taste
- Freshly ground pepper to taste

INSTRUCTIONS

1. Use a teaspoon of olive oil to brush strip steaks on both sides the season with freshly ground black pepper and salt. Repeat the same process with the other strip steak then set aside.
2. Place the steaks over the lower rack of wood pellet grill then set the temperature to about 225°F. Smoke the steaks for about an hour or until the internal temperature reaches 100°F
3. Remove from the grill when ready then let them stay warm as you preheat the wood pellet grill to 700°F.
4. Once the grill is heated, switch it to open flame cooking mode then remove the lower racks and replace with direct flame insert. Place back the grates on the grill at the lower position.
5. Sear the steaks as you use tongs to turn them until it develops a nice crust on the outside. Once cooked, transfer the steak strips to a cutting board then allow to rest for about 5 minutes.
6. Add a pinch of kosher salt to the meat then serve and enjoy.

SMOKED CORNED BEEF BRISKET

(COOKING TIME: 4 HOURS 10 MINUTES)

INGREDIENTS FOR **6** SERVINGS

- Corned beef brisket – 4 lb.
- Dijon or horseradish mustard
- Jeff's original rub
- Jeff's original barbecue sauce
- Foil pan or stainless steel

INSTRUCTIONS

1. Soak the corned beef brisket in cold water inside the fridge and keep changing the water after 30 minutes to remove the extra salt.
2. You can soak it for about 3 hours. You can then coat the entire beef brisket using horseradish mustard.
3. Liberally apply Jeff's original rub to all of the sides. You can pat the rub instead of massaging it into the meat.
4. Set smoker to 225°F with wood pellet smoke then place corned beef brisket over the smoker grate and let it smoke for about 3 hours or until the temperature of the thickest part reaches 140°F.
5. Make a sauce by mixing together Jeff's original barbecue sauce with Dijon then create a mustard pad at the pan's bottom and place the meat over the pad with the fat side up.
6. Brush it with more of the mustard sauce the cover with foil. Place it in a smoker and continue cooking for about one hour or until the temperature of the thickest part reaches 185°F.
7. Allow the meat to rest for about 30 minutes then slice it and serve.

EASY RIBS

(COOKING TIME: 4 HOURS 10 MINUTES)

INGREDIENTS FOR 5 SERVINGS

- Back Rib – 1 rack
- Pit boss sweet rib rub – 1 bottle

INSTRUCTIONS

1. Get the ribs off the packaging then pat to dry. Score the membrane using a knife then peel it off.
2. Use sweet pit boss rib rub to generously sprinkle the ribs on both of the sides then rub well.
3. Set up the smoker using wood pellets and heat to 250ºF.Once ready add the ribs the cook for about 4 hours or until the ribs become tender with the meat also pulling from the bone.
4. Serve and enjoy

SMOKED RIBEYE STEAKS

(COOKING TIME: 1 HOUR 10 MINUTES)

INGREDIENTS FOR 4 SERVINGS

- Ribeye steak – 4 lb.
- Favorite steak rub

INSTRUCTIONS

1. Get the pellet grill preheated to produce low smoke then allow ribeye to stay at room temperature for about 30 minutes.
2. Sprinkle your favorite steak rub then let it cook for about 30 minutes. Remove ribeye from the pellet grill then adjust the grill temperature to about 400°F
3. Place ribeye back on the pellet grill then sear each side for about 5 minutes.
4. Let it cook at desired temperature for about 20 minutes. Wrap ribeye using foil then allow to stay before slicing for about 10 minutes before slicing.
5. Serve and enjoy

SMOKED PRIME RIB

(COOKING TIME: 6 HOUR 20 MINUTES)

INGREDIENTS FOR 4 SERVINGS

- Prime rib roast
- Black pepper to taste
- Kosher salt to taste

INSTRUCTIONS

1. Pat the rib dry then wrap with twine.
2. Cover the rib with kosher salt liberally then refrigerate overnight.
3. Remove from the refrigerator then apply a good amount of black pepper.
4. Turn the pellet grill on to high smoke setting then allow it to stay for about 15 minutes. Place the prime rib over the grill then insert meat probe.
5. Allow it to cook until the internal temperature of the meat reaches 110°F.
6. Turn the smoker temperature to 400°F then let the meat continue to cook until the internal temperature reaches 125°F.
7. Remove meat from the grill then wrap into a foil. Let it stay in the foil for about 20 minutes until all of the juices settle.
8. Unwrap the top foil then pour juices from the foil into a bowl. Slice the meat then sprinkle with kosher salt.
9. Serve with the reserved juices and enjoy.

CHAPTER 2: PORK RECIPES

PEPPERCORN GRILLED PORK

(COOKING TIME: 1 HOUR 10 MINUTES)

INGREDIENTS FOR 4 SERVINGS

- Ground black peppercorns – 3 tablespoons
- Coriander see – 1 tablespoon
- Dry rub – 2 teaspoons
- Olive oil – 1 teaspoon
- Cumin – ¼ cup
- Chop bone-in – 4
- Sugar – 2 tablespoons
- Salt – 1 ½ teaspoon

INSTRUCTIONS

1. Start your pellet grill on smoke and the let the fire start for about 5 minutes. Get it preheated to about 450°F.
2. Combine the black peppercorns, cumin seeds, and coriander seeds into an iron skillet then place over medium heat and roast for about 8 minutes.
3. Allow the mixture to cool then grind finely in a blender and transfer to a bowl. Add sugar and salt to the mixture then combine.
4. Rub the spices mixture over the pork chops. Place an iron skillet over the grill then once hot, add olive oil and let it coat at the bottom of the skillet.
5. Sprinkle salt over the pork chops then add to the skillet as well. Ensure that there is sufficient space for each of the pork chops then cook them well.
6. Turn off the grill then serve and enjoy.

GRILLED PORK STEAK

(COOKING TIME: 1 HOUR 30 MINUTES)

INGREDIENTS FOR **4** SERVINGS

- Pork steaks – 4
- Grill AP rub – ¼ cup
- Grill BBQ sauce – ¼ cup
- Apple cider – 1 ½ cup
- Hot sauce – 2 teaspoon
- Dried thyme 2 teaspoon
- Maple syrup – 1 cup
- Sea salt – 1/3 cup
- Ice water – 1 ½ cup
- Water – 1 cup

INSTRUCTIONS

1. In a saucepan add a cup of water, 1/3 cup of maple syrup, salt and dried thyme then cook over medium heat for about 2 minutes or until the salt dissolves.
2. Remove it from heat then add ice water, cider and a teaspoon of hot sauce. Stir the mixture until the ice dissolves. You can then chill the brine to 45 degrees.
3. Place pork steaks into a zip-top bag then pour in the brine and seal. Allow it to res for about 2 hours in the refrigerator.
4. In a bowl, combine the remaining maple syrup, with the barbeque sauce and the hot sauce then set aside. Get the pellet grill preheated to about 300°F
5. Get the pork steaks off the brine then pat with paper towels. Grill the pork steak until the grill marks begin to appear on the first side then flip to grill the other side.
6. Once ready check if the internal temperature is at 160 degrees. In the last 10 minutes, brush pork steaks with syrup mixture after every 3 minutes as it cook.
7. Allow the steaks to rest for about 5 minutes then serve and enjoy.

EASY PORK STEAK

(COOKING TIME: 1 HOUR 30 MINUTES)

INGREDIENTS FOR 4 SERVINGS

- Pork steak
- Al purpose rub
- Gold N' Bold Sauce

INSTRUCTIONS

1. Begin by applying all-purpose rub on both the sides of pork steak. Get the pellet grill preheated to 275°F then place pork steaks over the grill,
2. Cook them for about 30 minutes on one side then flip to the other side and cook as you keep an eye on the hanging pieces to ensure they don't burn.
3. Check if the internal temperature is at 145°F then add some spice and drizzle with sauce to enhance flavor.
4. Allow to cool for about 5 minutes then serve and enjoy.

PORK BUTT

(COOKING TIME: 3 HOUR 10 MINUTES)

INGREDIENTS FOR **6** SERVINGS

Pork butt – 8 lbs.

INSTRUCTIONS

1. Trim and also score the pork butt then season with salt and preferred rub.
2. Prepare your Pellet grill then preheat to 225°F.
3. Cook the pork butt for about 3 hours on both side or until the internal temperature gets to 195°F
4. Allow it to cool for about 5 minutes then serve and enjoy.

PULLED PORK

(COOKING TIME: 8 HOUR 10 MINUTES)

INGREDIENTS FOR 6 SERVINGS

- Boston pork butt – 1 10lb
- Salt – ¾ cup
- Black pepper ¼ cup
- Grill AP Rub – 1/3 cup
- Aluminum foil

INSTRUCTIONS

1. Begin by preparing Boston pork butt, rinse it then pat it dry. Flip the fat cap up then rub salt all over the pork butt.
2. Coat it all over with pepper as well then allow the meat to stay at room temperature for while the wood pellet grill gets preheated to 275°F
3. Place pork on the wood pellet grill with the fat cap side facing upwards.
4. Cook it for about 4 hours, you can then turn it and let it cook for two more hours a 225°F.
5. Remove from the grill then wrap with two foil sheets. Cook them sealed for two more hours or until the internal temperature turns to 195°F in all of the parts.
6. Remove from the foil once the meat is cooked then place in a large bowl.
7. Add the cups of saved and rendered fat then use it to toss the meat before serving.
8. You can serve it with your preferred sauce.

CHAPTER 3: LAMB RECIPES

GARLIC RACK LAMB

(COOKING TIME: 3 HOUR 45 MINUTES)

INGREDIENTS FOR 4 SERVINGS

- Lamb Rack
- Basil – 1 teaspoon
- Oregano – 1 teaspoon
- Pepper mill – 10 cranks
- Marsala wine – 3 oz.
- Cram Sherry – 3 oz.
- Olive oil
- Madeira wine – 3 oz.
- Balsamic vinegar – 3 oz.
- Rosemary – 1 teaspoon

INSTRUCTIONS

1. Add all of the ingredients into a zip bag the mx well to form an emulsion.
2. Place the rack lamb into the bag the release all of the air as you rub the marinade all over the lamb.
3. Let it stay in the bag for about 45 minutes
4. Get the wood pellet grill preheated to 250°F then cook the lamb for 3 hours as you turn on both sides.
5. Ensure that the internal temperature is at 165°F before removing from the grill.
6. Allow to cool for a few minutes then serve and enjoy.

BRAISED LAMB SHANK

(COOKING TIME: 4 HOURS 20MINUTES)

INGREDIENTS FOR 6 SERVINGS

- Lamb shanks – 4
- Olive oil as required
- Beef broth – 1 cup
- Red wine – 1 cup
- Fresh thyme and sprigs – 4

INSTRUCTIONS

1. Season lamb shanks with prime rib rub then allow to rest.
2. Get the wood pellet grill temperature set to high then cook the lamb shanks for about 30 minutes.
3. Place the shanks directly on the grill gate then cook for another 20 minutes until browned on the outside.
4. Transfer the cooked lamb shanks into a Dutch oven then pour beef broth, the herbs and wine. Cover it with a fitting lid then place it back on the grill grate and allow it to cook at a reduced temperature of 325°F.
5. Brace the lamb shanks for about 3 hours or until the internal temperature gets to 180°F.
6. Remove the lid once ready then serve on a platter together with the accumulated juices and enjoy.

ROAST LAMB LEG

(COOKING TIME: 1 HOURS 30MINUTES)

INGREDIENTS FOR 6 SERVINGS

- Lamb leg with bone in – 7lbs
- Garlic cloves – 8
- Fresh rosemary sprigs – 2
- Fresh oregano – 1
- Juiced lemon – 1
- Olive oil – 6 tablespoon
- Freshly ground black pepper to taste
- Kosher salt to taste

INSTRUCTIONS

1. Use a knife to make a few slits in the leg the on a board mince together oregano, garlic and rosemary.
2. Stuff the minced mixture into each of the slits then place the lamb inside a roasting pan.
3. Rub the lamb with some lemon juice and olive oil then then cover using a plastic wrap and refrigerate for about 8 hours or overnight.
4. Remove from the refrigerator then let the lamb get to room temperature. Season with ground black pepper and salt then get the wood pellet grill preheated to 400°F with lid closed for about 15 minutes.
5. Roast the lamb for about 30 minutes then reduce the heat to about 350°F and continue cooking until the internal temperature of the lamb gets to 140°F.
6. Once the lamb is ready, transfer to a cutting board then allow it to rest for about 15 minutes.
7. Slice and enjoy

LAMB LOLLIPOPS

(COOKING TIME: 1 HOURS 30MINUTES)

INGREDIENTS FOR 4 SERVINGS

- Lamb chops – 6
- Olive oil – 2 tablespoon
- Peeled and seeded mango – 1
- Habanero pepper – ½ seeded and chopped
- Freshly ground black pepper – ½ teaspoon
- Kosher salt – ½ teaspoon
- Freshly chopped cilantro – 3 sprigs
- Fresh lime juice – 1 tablespoon
- Chopped fresh mint – 2 tablespoon
- Pepper freshly cracked – ½ teaspoon
- Salt – 1 teaspoon

INSTRUCTIONS

1. Add all of the ingredients for chutney into a food processor then pulse up to desired consistency.
2. Start the wood pellet grill on smoke as you leave the lid open until the fire comes up. Set the temperature to cook at high for about 15 minutes.
3. Place the lamb pops over the grill grate then cook for about 30 minutes or until the internal temperature that's inserted at the thickest part of the lamb pop reads 130°F.
4. Remove from the grill then allow to stay for about 10 minutes.
5. Sprinkle with some freshly chopped mint then serve and enjoy.

ROASTED LEG OF LAMB

(COOKING TIME: 1 HOURS 30MINUTES)

INGREDIENTS FOR 8 SERVINGS

- Leg of lamb with bone in – 8 lb.
- Crushed garlic – 1 tablespoon
- Cloves garlic – 4
- Sprigs rosemary – 4 cut in pieces
- Lemons – 2
- Salt and pepper to taste

INSTRUCTIONS

1. Combine crushed garlic and olive oil together then rub the mixture over the leg of lamb.
2. Use a small knife to make deep perforations of about ¾ inch into the lamb then stuff in garlic and rosemary sprigs to the perforations.
3. Zest juice lemons then spread the juice all over the lamb. Season the lamb with salt and pepper.
4. Set the temperature of the wood pellet grill to high as you preheat for about 15 minutes. Place the leg of lamb over the grill the cook for about 30 minutes.
5. Reduce the grill temperature to about 350°F then cook for about one hour or until the internal temperature gets to 130°F
6. Remove the leg of lamb from the grill then let it rest for about 15 minutes.
7. Carve the meat then enjoy.

CHAPTER 4: FISH RECIPES

GARLIC SALMON

(COOKING TIME: 30 MINUTES)

INGREDIENTS FOR 4 SERVINGS

- Salmon fillet with skin on – 3 lb.
- Minced garlic – 2 tablespoon
- Minced parsley – ½ tablespoon
- Lemon wedges for serving
- Olive oil – ¼ cup
- Fin and feather rub

INSTRUCTIONS

1. Line the baking sheet with parchment paper then place salmon with the skin side facing down.
2. Season the fillet with fin and feather rub then in a bowl, combine together parsley, garlic and olive oil then set aside.
3. Get the wood pellet grill preheated to high for about 15 minutes with the lid closed.
4. Brush garlic using garlic mixture then transfer to the grill. Cook it for 25 minutes or until the internal temperature reaches 140°F or until the fish begins to easily flake.
5. Once ready, remove from the grill then brush it with the remaining garlic mixture and serve together with the lemon wedges.

WHOLE RED SNAPPER

(COOKING TIME: 25 MINUTES)

INGREDIENTS FOR 4 SERVINGS

- Whole red snapper – 1
- Olive oil – 2 tablespoons
- Bunch of watercress - 1 trimmed and washed
- Cherry peppers – 2 thinly sliced
- Scallions – 3 thinly sliced
- Chopped cilantro – 2 tablespoon
- Kosher salt – ½ tablespoon
- Black pepper – 1 teaspoon
- Melted butter – ¼ cup
- Harissa – ¼ cup
- Fish sauce – ¼ teaspoon
- Olive oil – ¼ cup
- Salt and pepper to taste

INSTRUCTIONS

1. Combine harissa and melted butter into a medium bowl. Get the wood pellet grill preheated with lid closed for about 15 minutes.
2. Coat fish exterior with olive oil then season with salt and pepper.
3. Place it directly over the grill then brush it with harissa and butter mixture. You can then cook it for 20 minutes,
4. As the fish cooks, you can also prepare salad. In a bowl mix together lime juice, fish sauce, brown sugar, salt and pepper. Whisk it together the add olive oil.
5. In another bowl combine together the watercress, scallions, peppers, cilantro and mint.
6. Flip the fish then brush it with harissa butter mixture then close the lid and cook for about 15 minutes or until the temperature gets to 145°F.
7. Remove fish from the grill once ready then place on a serving platter. Drizzle the greens with the dressing then season with salt and pepper to taste.
8. Add salad over the fish then drizzle with the remaining dressing.
9. Enjoy

ROASTED HALIBUT

(COOKING TIME: 30 MINUTES)

INGREDIENTS FOR 4 SERVINGS

- Fish fillets – 4 (4oz)
- Olive oil
- Freshly ground pepper
- Kosher salt
- Lemons cut into slices – 2
- Kernels of corn
- Asparagus spears – 16
- Finely chopped 2 tablespoon
- Parchment paper

INSTRUCTIONS

1. Get the wood pellet grill preheated to high for about 15 minutes with lid closed.
2. Cut parchment paper into four pieces of 18" long then place the fish fillet at the center of the parchment paper.
3. Season it with salt and pepper then drizzle with some olive oil. Place three slices of lemon juice over the fillet to cover the fish.
4. Sprinkle asparagus, tomatoes, and corn around the fish then drizzle with olive oil as you also season with a pinch of salt and pepper.
5. Bring the sides of parchment paper together then fold the edges together to create an inch seal. Continue with folding it down tightly over the vegetables and the fish.
6. You can refrigerate it for about 4 hours then remove from the fridge and cook for about 20 minutes or until the fish is puffed up and lightly browned.
7. Transfer each of the packets to a platter then let it stay for about 15 minutes.
8. Remove the parchment paper then sprinkle the fish with herbs.
9. Serve and enjoy

CHAPTER 5: SEAFOOD RECIPES

SHRIMP

(COOKING TIME: 15 MINUTES)

INGREDIENTS FOR 2 SERVINGS

- Shrimp – 2 lb.
- Brown sugar – 1 tablespoon
- Smoked paprika 1 tablespoon
- Garlic powder – 1 teaspoon
- Ground thyme – ¼ teaspoon
- Ground cayenne – ¼ teaspoon
- Sea salt – 1 teaspoon
- Zest of lime
- Olive oil 3 tablespoon

INSTRUCTIONS

1. In a bowl mix together lime zest, spices and salt then combine. Place shrimp into a bowl then drizzle with olive oil. Add spice mixture then toss well to combine as you also ensure every shrimp is touched with the mixture.
2. When ready for cooking, get the wood pellet grill preheated for about 15 minutes with the lid closed. Set the temperature to 450°F
3. Arrange shrimp over the grill then cook for about 3 minutes on each side.
4. Serve the shrimp with fresh cilantro, lime wedges, hot pepper sauce and mint.
5. Enjoy

GRILLED LOBSTER TAILS

(COOKING TIME: 25 MINUTES)

INGREDIENTS FOR 2 SERVINGS

- Lobster tails – 2 10oz
- Butter – 8 tablespoon
- Lemon juice – 2 tablespoon
- Paprika – 1 teaspoon
- Garlic salt – ¼ teaspoon
- Old bay seasoning – ¼ teaspoon
- Freshly ground black pepper – ¼ teaspoon
- Freshly chopped parsley – 2 tablespoon

INSTRUCTIONS

1. Prepare the lobster by cutting through the tough shell towards the tail. Use fingers to pry meat from the shell as you keep it attached at the base.
2. Make a slit on the meat right down through the middle so as to open it up then place the lobster over a rimmed baking sheet.
3. Place a saucepan over medium heat then melt butter. Whisk in old bay seasoning, garlic salt, lemon juice, pepper and parsley.
4. Pour a tablespoon of butter mixture over the lobster tail as you keep the butter mixture that's remaining warm.
5. When ready to start cooking, begin by preheating the wood pellet grill to high for about 15 minutes with the lid closed.
6. Remove lobster tails then arrange them over the grill grate. Cook them for about 30 minutes or until the meat turns opaque and white.
7. Transfer to a platter the lobster tails then serve it with the butter mixture that was reserved.
8. Serve and enjoy

SMOKED TROUT

(COOKING TIME: 25 MINUTES)

INGREDIENTS FOR 4 SERVINGS

- Rainbow trout – 8
- Black pepper – 1 tablespoon
- Soy sauce – 2 tablespoon
- Brown sugar – ½ cup
- Water – 1 gal
- Salt – 1/4cup

INSTRUCTIONS

1. Clean the trouts then open then up.
2. To prepare the brine, in a bowl mix together brown sugar, water, soy sauce, salt and pepper. Brine the trout then refrigerate for about an hour.
3. Get the wood pellet grill preheated for about 15 minutes with the lid closed then set the temperature to 225°F.
4. Get the trout off the brine then pat to dry. Place trout directly over the grill grate then cook for about 2 hours depending on how thick the rout are.
5. You will know that the trout is done when it becomes flaky and turns opaque.
6. Serve and enjoy.

CHAPTER 6: POULTRY RECIPES

BBQ HALF CHICKEN

(COOKING TIME: 1 HOUR 30 MINUTES)

INGREDIENTS FOR **4** SERVINGS

- Young fresh chicken – 1 (3 ½ lb.)
- BBQ sauce
- Shandy rub

INSTRUCTIONS

1. Place chicken onto a cutting board with the breast side facing down then cut along the backbone side right from the neck all the way to the tail.
2. Repeat with the other backbone then open the chicken up and slice accordingly.
3. Season the chicken with shandy rub then let it rest.
4. Prepare the wood pellet grill by preheating it to 375°F with the lid closed for about 15 minutes.
5. Place the chicken over the grill directly then cook for one hour 20 minutes.
6. Once ready, brush the chicken skin with BBQ sauce all over then cook for an extra 10 minutes.
7. Remove from the grill then allow to rest for about 5 minutes.
8. Serve and enjoy

THANKSGIVING TURKEY

(COOKING TIME: 1 HOUR 30 MINUTES)

INGREDIENTS FOR **8** SERVINGS

- Turkey – 1 (20lb)
- Softened butter – ½ lb.
- Sprigs thyme – 8
- Minced cloves garlic – 6
- Sprig rosemary rough chop – 1
- Cracked black pepper 1 tablespoon
- Kosher salt – ½ tablespoon

INSTRUCTIONS

1. In a bowl mix together minced garlic, thyme leaves, butter, chopped rosemary, kosher salt and black pepper.
2. Prepare the turkey by creating a pocket for stuffing butter hub mixture. You can do that by separating skin from breast.
3. Cover the breast entirely with up to 1/4" thickness of the butter mixture.
4. You can then season it with black pepper and kosher salt.
5. Preheat the wood pellet grill to 300oF with the lid closed for about 15 minutes.
6. Place turkey over the grill then cook it for about 4 hours. Once ready, check for the desired internal temperature to be at 175oF. The turkey will still cook even after being taken off the grill with a temperature of 165oF at the breast.
7. Allow it to rest for about 15 minutes then carve and enjoy.

ROASTED TERIYAKI WINGS

(COOKING TIME: 1 HOUR 30 MINUTES)

INGREDIENTS FOR 8 SERVINGS

- Large chicken wings – 2 ½ lbs.
- Soy sauce – ½ cup
- Brown sugar – ¼ cup
- Rice wine vinegar – 2 tablespoon
- Scallions – 2
- Minced cloves garlic – 1
- Sesame oil – 2 teaspoon
- Smashed fresh ginger – 2 tablespoons
- Lightly roasted sesame seeds – 1 tablespoon

INSTRUCTIONS

1. Cut the chicken wings into pieces as you discard the wing tips.
2. Transfer the chicken wings into a resealable plastic bag. For the marinade, combine water, brown sugar, scallions, vinegar, sesame oil, ginger and garlic into a bowl then cook over medium heat for about 10 minutes.
3. Let the marinade cool completely then pour it on the chicken wings. Get the bag sealed then refrigerate overnight or for a number of hours.
4. Drain the wings of the marinade and set aside.
5. Get the wood pellet grill preheated to 350ºF for about 15 minutes with the lid closed.
6. Cook the chicken wings for one hour or until the skin turns crisp and brown.
7. Remove from the grill once ready then sprinkle with the sesame seeds.
8. Serve and enjoy

BBQ CHICKEN BREASTS

(COOKING TIME: 30 MINUTES)

INGREDIENTS FOR **6** SERVINGS

- Boneless and skinless chicken breast – 6
- BBQ sauce – 1 ½
- Chopped parsley to garnish
- Salt and pepper to taste

INSTRUCTIONS

1. Place chicken breasts and a cup of BBQ into a Ziploc bag then allow it to marinate overnight.
2. Get the wood pellet grill heated to high for about 15 minutes with the lid closed.
3. Remove chicken from the marinade then season using salt and pepper.
4. Place the chicken over the grill directly then cook for about 15 minutes on every side. Once ready, check to ascertain that the internal temperature is at 150°F
5. Brush chicken with the remaining sauce while still on the grill then continue cooking for 10 more minutes or until the internal temperature gets to 165°F
6. Remove from the grill then allow to stay for about 5 minutes before you serve. Sprinkle the chicken with some chopped parsley then serve and enjoy.

ROASTED BUFFALO WING

(COOKING TIME: 1 HOUR 10 MINUTES)

INGREDIENTS FOR 6 SERVINGS

- Chicken wings – 4 lbs.
- Cornstarch – 1 tablespoon
- Spicy mustard – ¼ cup
- Unsalted butter – 6 tablespoon
- Red hot sauce – ½ cup
- Chicken rub

INSTRUCTIONS

1. Get the wood pellet grill preheated to 375°F with the lid closed for about 15 minutes.
2. Dry the chicken wings using a paper towel then place them in a bowl. Sprinkle the wings with cornstarch, salt and chicken rub then mix to coat well.
3. Once the grill is heated, place the wings over the grill then cook for about 30 minutes as you turn it halfway while you cook.
4. Check the wings internal temperature to be at 165°F
5. For the sauce, add red hot sauce in a bowl together with butter and mustard then whisk together to combine as you heat over a stove top.
6. Keep the sauce warm as the wings cook then once done, use the sauce to coat the wings then cook for 15 more minutes.
7. Serve the wings together with blue cheese dressing and enjoy.

CHAPTER 7: VEGETABLE RECIPES

GRILLED ZUCCHINI

(COOKING TIME: 1 HOUR 10 MINUTES)

INGREDIENTS FOR 4 SERVINGS

- Olive oil – 2 tablespoons
- Medium zucchini – 4
- Cherry vinegar – 1 tablespoons
- Springs thyme leaves pulled 2
- Salt and pepper to taste

INSTRUCTIONS

1. Clean zucchini then cut the ends off. Cut each of the zucchini into half then split each half into thirds.
2. Mix the other ingredients into a Ziploc bag then toss to combine well for the zucchini to coat.
3. Once ready to cook, get the wood pellet grill preheated with the lid closed for about 15 minutes.
4. Remove the spears then place over the grill with the cut side facing down.
5. Let it cook for about 4 minutes on each side or until the zucchini becomes tender and with grill marks.
6. Remove from then grill then serve with some more thyme leaves as desired.

GRILLED SUGAR SNAP PEAS

(COOKING TIME: 20 MINUTES)

INGREDIENTS FOR 4 SERVINGS

- Sugar snap peas – 2 lb.
- Olive oil – 2 tablespoon
- Butter – 2 tablespoon
- Shallots thinly sliced – 2 medium
- Minced clove garlic
- Bourbon – ¼ cup
- Maple syrup – 2 tablespoon
- Salt and pepper to taste

INSTRUCTIONS

1. Get the wood pellet grill preheated to 3500F for about 15 minutes and with lid closed.
2. In a bowl, mix together olive oil, peas, salt and pepper then toss to mix well.
3. Place a tray over the grill to prevent the peas from falling over then cook for about 10 minutes or until tender and lightly browned.
4. While the peas is cooking, add butter to a skillet over medium heat then add garlic and shallot.
5. Sauté for about 5 minutes or until tender. Deglaze with bourbon then continue cooking until the quantity is reduced to half.
6. Add maple syrup into the mixture alongside salt and pepper to taste then set aside.
7. Toss the grilled sugar snap peas with the maple bourbon mixture then serve and enjoy.

HONEY GLAZED ASPARAGUS WITH GRILLED CARROTS

(COOKING TIME: 30 MINUTES)

INGREDIENTS FOR 4 SERVINGS

- Pencil sized asparagus - 1 bunch with trimmed ends
- Whole carrots – 1 lb. with tops
- Olive oil – 2 tablespoons
- Honey – 2 tablespoons
- Lemon zest
- Sea salt as required

INSTRUCTIONS

1. Get all of the vegetables rinsed with cold water then pat to dry.
2. Drizzle asparagus using sea salt and olive oil. Drizzle carrots as well with honey then lightly sprinkle sea salt.
3. Get the wood pellet grill preheated for 15 minutes with lid closed then roast the carrots and asparagus for about 30 minutes or until done as desired.
4. Remove from the grill when ready then top with some lemon zest and enjoy.

BRUSSELS SPROUTS

(COOKING TIME: 50 MINUTES)

INGREDIENTS FOR **6** SERVINGS

- Brussels sprouts – 2lbs
- Medium sliced onion - 1
- Salt and pepper to taste
- Olive oil

INSTRUCTIONS

1. Get the wood pellet grill preheated for 15 minutes to 450°F
2. Slice onion into half and the ¼ inch then add into a bowl. Slice the brussels sprouts into half then add into the bowl.
3. Drizzle the mixture with olive oil then season with salt and pepper. Toss well to coat then pour into a baking pan.
4. Place the baking pan on grill then roast the mixture for 30 minutes while mixing when halfway done.
5. Serve immediately and enjoy.

CHAPTER 8: SMOKING TIPS

TYPES OF SMOKERS

ELECTRIC SMOKERS

The electric smoker is the best smoker because it is very simple to use. Just set it, put your food in it and leave the rest of the work to the smoker. There is nothing an electric smoker can't grill, be it seafood, poultry, meat, cheese or bread. It requires little attention unlike other smokers like filling water bin, lighting wood or charcoal and checking on fuel frequently. Yes, unlike traditional smoker, electric smoker just need 2 to 4 ounce of wood chips that turns out a delicious and flavorful smoky food. Furthermore, they maintain cooking temperature really well. On the other hand, it sleek and stylish look and small size make it appropriate if you are living in an apartment or condo. Due to their simpler functions and hassle-free cooking, the electric smoker is a good choice for beginner cooks who want to get started with smoking food.

GAS SMOKERS

Gas smokers or propane smoker are much like a gas grill using propane as a fuel. Therefore, the heat for cooking remains consistent and steady. Furthermore, gas smokers are as easy to use, just set the temperature and walk away. However, frequent checks need to be done to make sure fuel doesn't run out. It isn't a big issue but one should keep in mind. And the best part, a gas smoker can be used when there is no electricity or when you need an oven. A gas smoker can take up to cooking temperature to 450 degrees, making this smoker flexible to be used as an oven. Another fantastic feature of gas smoker is its portability so they can use anywhere. Just pack it and take it along with you on your camping trips or other outdoor adventures.

CHARCOAL SMOKERS

Nothing can beat the flavor charcoal gives to your food. Its best flavor just simply can't match with any other smoker flavor. Unfortunately, setting a charcoal smoker, tuning fuel, maintaining cooking temperature and checking food can be a pain and you might burn the food. Not to worry, these hassles of a charcoal smoker does go away with practice and experience. Therefore, a charcoal smoker suits perfectly for serious grillers and barbecue purist who want flavors.

PELLET SMOKERS

Pellet smokers are making a surge due to their best feature of a pallet of maintaining a consistent temperature. It contains an automated system to drop pallets which frees the cook to monitor fuel level. The addition of thermostat gives the user the complete control the cooking temperature and grilling of food under ideal condition. In addition, the smoking food uses the heat from hardwood which gives food a delicious flavor. The only downside of pallet smoker is their high cost between the ranges of $100 to %600.

TYPES OF SMOKER WOODS

Smoker wood is an important element which you need to decide correctly to cook a delicious smoked food. The reason is that smoker chips of woods impart different flavors on the food you are cooking in the smoker. Therefore, you should know which smoker wood should be used to create a delicious smoked food. Here is the lowdown of smoker woods and which food is best with them.

1- Alder: A lighter smoker wood with natural sweetness.
   Best to smoke: Any fish especially salmon, poultry and game birds.
2- Maple: This smoker wood has a mild and sweet flavor. In addition, its sweet smoke gives the food a dark appearance. For better flavor, use it as a combination with alder, apple or oak smoker woods.
   Best to smoke: Vegetables, cheese, and poultry.
3- Apple: A mild fruity flavor smoker wood with natural sweetness. When mixed with oak smoker wood, it gives a great flavor to food. Let food smoke for several hours as the smoke takes a while to permeate the food with the flavors.
   Best to smoke: Poultry, beef, pork, lamb, and seafood.
4- Cherry: This smoker wood is an all-purpose fruity flavor wood for any type of meat. Its smoke gives the food a rich, mahogany color. Try smoking by mixing it with alder, oak, pecan and hickory smoker wood.
   Best to smoke: Chicken, turkey, ham, pork, and beef.
5- Oak: Oakwood gives a medium flavor to food which is stronger compared to apple wood and cherry wood and lighter compared to hickory. This versatile smoker wood works well blended with hickory, apple, and cherry woods.
   Best to smoke: Sausages, brisket, and lamb.
6- Peach and Pear: Both smoker woods are similar to each other. They give food a subtle light and fruity flavor with the addition of natural sweetness.
   Best to smoke: Poultry, pork and game birds.
7- Hickory: Hickory wood infuses a strong sweet and bacon flavor into the food, especially meat cuts. Don't over smoke with this wood as it can turn the taste of food bitter.

Best to smoke: Red meat, poultry, pork shoulder, ribs.

8- Pecan: This sweet smoker wood lends the food a rich and nutty flavor. Use it with Mesquite wood to balance its sweetness.
Best to smoke: Poultry, pork.

9- Walnut: This strong flavored smoker wood is often used as a mixing wood due to its slightly bitter flavor. Use walnut wood with lighter smoke woods like pecan wood or apple wood.
Best to smoke: Red meat and game birds.

10- Grape: Grape wood chips give a sweet berry flavor to food. It's best to use these wood chips with apple wood chips.
Best to smoke: Poultry

11- Mulberry: Mulberry wood chips is similar to apple wood chips. It adds natural sweetness and gives berry finish to the food.
Best to smoke: Ham and Chicken.

12- Mesquite: Mesquite wood chips flavor is earthy and slightly harsh and bitter. It burns fast and strongly hot. Therefore, don't use it for longer grilling.

Best to smoke: Red meat, dark meat.

THE DIFFERENT TYPES OF CHARCOAL AND THEIR BENEFITS

Charcoal is one of the efficient fuels for smoking. It burns hot, with more concentrated fire. Smoking food with charcoal is awesome. Though lighting charcoals, regulating airflows and controlling the heat is always a challenge, however, the excellent taste of food is worth this challenge. But, keep in mind that not all charcoals are equal and selecting one is a matter of preference.

LUMP CHARCOAL:

Lump charcoal or hardwood is the first choice of griller as a better fuel source. It is basically made by burning wood logs in an underground pit for a few days. As a result, water, sap, and other substances in log burn out, leaving behind a pure char or lump charcoal. This charcoal burns pure, hot and efficiently. They burn hotter in the beginner and burn cooler by the end. Therefore, lump charcoal is a good choice for broiling quickly or searing food at intense heat. In addition, the lump char also add the aroma of wood smoke into the food which takes the taste to another level of gastronomical heaven. Since, lump charcoal cool its fire in 30 minutes, replenish fire to maintain the temperature which takes only 5 to 10 minutes by adding few unlit coals. It's recommended to use lump charcoal with a combination of wood chips like maple, oak or hickory and refuel this wood chips every 40 minutes during smoking food.

CHARCOAL BRIQUETTES:

Charcoal briquettes are actually crushed charcoal. The major benefit of using this natural charcoal is its even shape and size. This is done by adding chemical binders and fillers like coal dust and compressing into a pillow shape. Therefore, creating a bed of coals is very easy with charcoal briquettes which are quite hard with uneven and irregular charcoals. The only downside is that they burn very quickly, more than lump charcoal. This creates a short window for smoking food, therefore, more briquettes need to add during grilling.

THE DIFFERENCE BETWEEN BARBECUING A MEAT AND SMOKING IT?

There are two main ways to cook meat that has become an increasingly popular cooking method: smoking or barbecuing. They are both different and require different cooking equipment, temperature, and timing. Following is the full comparison between smoking and barbecue.

BARBECUING MEAT:

Barbecue is a slow cooking, indirectly over low heat between 200 to 250 degrees F. Therefore, it is best suited for beef brisket, whole pig, turkeys or pork shoulder. These animals tend to have tough muscles which need slow cooking over low heat to get a moist and tender meat. It turns out an extremely tender and flavorful meat. The best example of a perfect barbecue is falling of meat off the bones. During the barbecue, the fuel needs to be filled frequently but do this quickly, as lifting lid of burner exposes meat to air which can turn it dry.

For barbecuing meat, the grill needs to be preheated until hot. For this light enough charcoals or bкisquettes so that their fire turns down for cooking. In the meantime, season meat and then when grill reaches to perfect cooking temperature, place seasoned meat on it. Having grill on perfect temperature is essential as meat won't stick to grilling grate.

Equipment: Fire pit, grill or a charcoal burner with lid.

Fueling: Lump wood charcoal, charcoal briquettes or wood chips combination like apple. Cherry and oak wood chips.

Best to smoke: A big cut of meats like Briskets, whole chicken, sausages, jerky, pork, and ribs.

Temperature: 190 to 300 degrees F

Timing: 2 hours to a day long.

SMOKING MEAT:

Smoking is one of the oldest cooking technique dating back to the first people living in caves. It was traditionally a food preservation method and with the time, its popularity never died. Smoking is a related process of barbecue. It's the best cooking method to bring out the rich and deep flavor of meat that tastes heavenly when meat is smoked until it comes off the bone.

During smoking, food is cooked below 200 degrees F cooking temperature. Therefore, smoking food requires a lot of time and patience. It infuses woody flavor into the meat and turns a silky and fall-of-bone meat. There are three ways to smoke food, cold smoke, hot smoke and adding liquid smoke. In these three types of smoking methods, liquid smoke is becoming increasingly common. Its main advantage is that smoke flavor is controlled. In addition, the effect of liquid smoke on meat is immediate.

There is another smoking method which called water smoking. It uses water smoker which is specifically designed to incorporate water in the smoking process. The water helps in controlling the temperature of smoker which is great for large cut meats for long hours.

Equipment: A closed container or high-tech smoker.

Fueling: The container will need an external source for a smoke. Wood chips are burn to add smoky flavor to the meat. However, the frequent check should be made to monitor and adjust temperature for smoking.

Best to smoke: A big cut of meats like Briskets, whole chicken, pork, and ribs.

Temperature: 68 to 176 degrees F

Timing: 1 hour to 2 weeks

THE CORE DIFFERENCE BETWEEN COLD AND HOT SMOKING

There are two ways to smoke meat that is cold smoking and hot smoking. In cold smoking, meat is cooked between 68 to 86 degrees F until smoked but moist. It is a good choice to smoke meat like chicken breast, steak, beef, pork chops, salmon, and cheese. The cold smoking concern with adding flavor to the meat rather than cooking. Therefore, when the meat is cold smoked, it should be cured, baked or steamed before serving.

On the other hand, hot smoking cooks the meat completely, in addition, to enhance its flavor. Therefore, meat should be a cook until its internal temperature is between 126 to 176 degrees F. Don't let meat temperature reach 185 degrees F as at this temperature, meat shrinks or buckles. Large meat cuts like brisket, ham, ribs and pulled pork turns out great when hot smoked.

THE CORE ELEMENTS OF SMOKING

There are six essential elements of smoking.

1- Wood chips: Chip of woods are used as a fuel either alone or in combination with charcoals. In addition, these chips add fantastic flavor to the meat. Therefore, chips of wood should only be used which suits best to the meat.

2- Smoker: There are basically four choices from which a smoker should be the pick. The choices are an electric smoker, charcoal smoker, gas smoker and pellet smoker. Each has its own advantages and downsides.

3- Smoking time: Smoking time is essential for perfect of meat cuts. It is actually the time when the internal temperature reaches its desired values. It may take 2 hours up to more than two weeks.

4- Meat: The star of the show is meat that needs to be more tender, juicy and flavorful after smoking. Make sure, the meat you sure has fat trimmed from it. In addition, it should complement the wood of chips.

5- Rub: Rubs, mixture or salt and spices, add sweetness and heat to the meat. They should be prepared in such a way that all types of flavor should be balanced in the meat.

6- Mops: Mops or liquid is often used during smoking meat. It adds a little bit flavor to the meat and maintains tenderness and moisture throughout the smoking process.

THE BASIC PREPARATIONS FOR SMOKING MEAT

CHOOSING SMOKER

The major and foremost step is to choose a smoker. You can invest in any type of the smoker: charcoal smoker, gas smoker or an electric smoker. A charcoal smoker runs for a long time and maintain steadier heat in the smoker and give meat pure flavors. A good choice for beginner cook for smoking meat is a gas smoker where there is no need to monitor temperature but it comes with a downside that meat won't have much flavor compared to charcoal. On the other hand, the simplest, easiest and popular smoker is an electric smoker. Cooking with electric smoker involves only two-step: turn it on, put meat in it and walk away. Read more details about smokers in the section "type of smokers".

CHOOSING FUEL

Wood chips add a unique flavor to the meat, therefore, select that wood chips that would enhance the taste of meat. Some wood of chips have a stronger flavor, some have mild while others are just enough to be alone for smoking. Check out the section titled "types of smoker wood" to get to know and decide chips of wood that will complement your meat.

TYPE OF SMOKING METHOD

You have two choices to smoke meat, either using wet smoking, dry smoking, liquid smoke or water smoking. Read the section "The core difference between cold and hot smoking" to find out differences between each. In addition, go through smoking meat portion in the section "the difference between barbecuing a meat and smoking it".

SOAKING CHIPS OF WOOD

Wood chips need to soak in order to last longer for fueling smoking. The reason is dry wood that burns quickly and this means, adding fuel to the smoker which can result in dry smoked meat. There isn't any need of using wood chips when smoking for a shorter time. Prepare wood chips by soaking them in water for at least 4 hours before starting smoking. Then drain chips and wrap and seal them in an aluminium foil. Use toothpick or fork for poking holes into the wood chips bag.

SET SMOKER

Each type of smoker have its own way to start smoking. For wood or charcoal smoker, first, light up half of the charcoals and wait until their flame goes down. Then add remaining charcoal and wood chips if using. Wait they are lighted and giving heat completely, then push charcoal aside and place meat on the other side of grilling grate. This is done to make sure that meat is indirectly smoked over low heat. Continue adding charcoal and/or soaked wood chips into the smoker.

For gas/propane or electric smoker, just turn it on according to manufacturer guideline and then add soaked wood chips into chip holder and fill water receptacle if a smoker has one. Either make use of the incorporated thermostat or buy your own to monitor the internal temperature of the smoker. When smoker reaches to desired preheated temperature, add meat to it.

SELECTING MEAT FOR SMOKING

Choose the type of meat which tastes good with a smoky flavor. Following meat goes well for smoking.

Beef: ribs, brisket and corned beef.

Pork: spare ribs, roast, shoulder, and ham.

Poultry: whole chicken, whole turkey, and big game hens.

Seafood: Salmon, scallops, trout, and lobster.

GETTING MEAT READY

Prepare meat according to the recipe. Sometimes meat is cured, marinated or simply seasoned with the rub. These preparation methods ensure smoked meat turn out flavorful, tender and extremely juicy.

Brine is a solution to treating poultry, pork or ham. It involves dissolving brine ingredients in water poured into a huge container and then adding meat to it. Then let soak for at least 8 hours and after that, rinse it well and pat dry before you begin smoking.

Marinate treat beef or briskets and add flavors to it. It's better to make deep cuts in meat to let marinate ingredients deep into it. Drain meat or smoke it straightaway.

Rubs are commonly used to treat beef, poultry or ribs. They are actually a combination of salt and many spices, rubbed generously all over the meat. Then the meat is left to rest for at least 2 hours or more before smoking it.

Before smoking meat, make sure it is at room temperature. This ensures meat is cooked evenly and reach its internal temperature at the end of smoking time.

PLACING MEAT INTO THE SMOKER

Don't place the meat directly over heat into the smoker because the main purpose of smoking is cooking meat at low temperature. Set aside your fuel on one side of the smoker and place meat on the other side and let cook.

Smoking time: The smoking time of meat depends on the internal temperature. For this, use a meat thermometer and insert it into the thickest part of the meat. The smoking time also varies with the size of meat. Check recipes to determine the exact smoking time for the meat.

BASTING MEAT

Some recipes call for brushing meat with thin solutions, sauces or marinade. This step not only makes meat better in taste, it also helps to maintain moisture in meat through the smoking process. Read recipe to check out if basting is necessary.

Taking out meat: When the meat reaches its desired internal temperature, remove it from the smoker. Generally, poultry should be removed from smoker when its internal temperature reaches to 165 degrees F. For ground meats, ham, and pork, the internal temperature should be 160 degrees F. 145 degrees F is the internal temperature for chops, roast, and steaks.

CONCLUSION

As you can see from these recipes, the world of smoking is only as limited as your imagination! Sweet, savory, vegetable, mineral, meat- you can smoke almost anything. As you get more comfortable with these recipes, feel free to start experimenting on your own. The basic principles hold true, but your own taste buds can drive you. Good luck, and happy smoking!

GET YOUR FREE GIFT

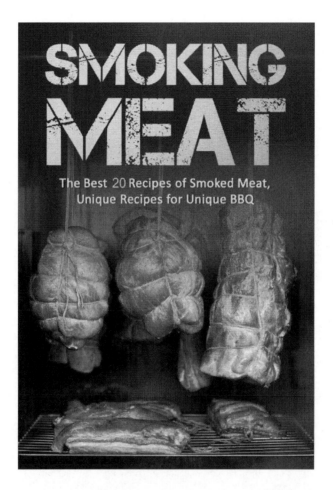

Subscribe to our Mail List and get your FREE copy of the book

'Smoking Meat: The Best 20 Recipes of Smoked Meat, Unique Recipes for Unique BBQ'

https://tiny.cc/smoke20

OTHER BOOKS BY DANIEL MURRAY

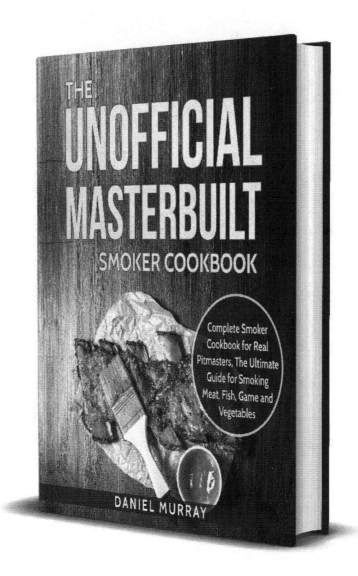

https://www.amazon.com/gp/product/B07JVHZ4PJ

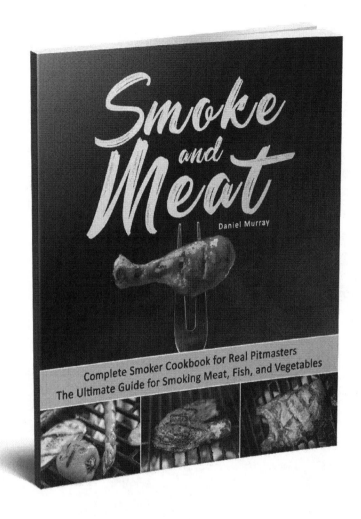

https://www.amazon.com/dp/B07D8NFZ3F

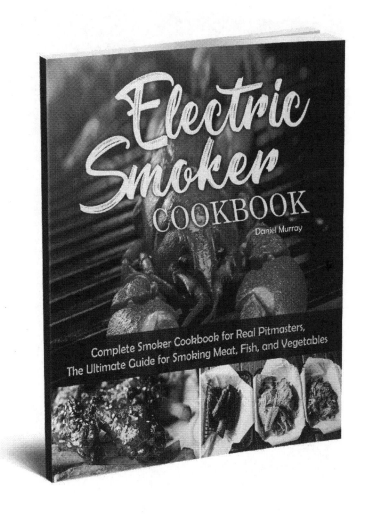

HTTPS://WWW.AMAZON.COM/DP/B07DKZ3NSK

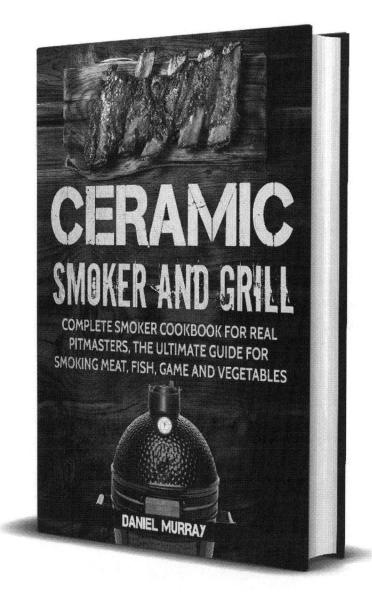

HTTPS://WWW.AMAZON.COM/DP/B07GSKRLB8

Made in the USA
Columbia, SC
10 December 2019